PowerKiDS
Readers
AMERICAN SYMBOLS

THE STATUE OF LIBERTY

Joe Gaspar

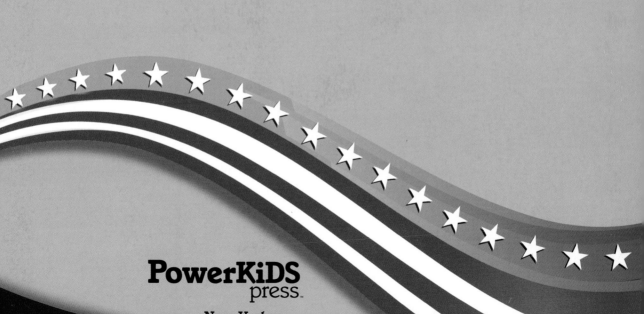

PowerKiDS
press.

New York

Published in 2014 by The Rosen Publishing Group, Inc.
29 East 21st Street, New York, NY 10010

First Edition

Editor: Amelie von Zumbusch
Book Design: Colleen Bialecki

Photo Credits: Cover ag-photos/Shutterstock.com; p. 5 upthebanner/Shutterstock.com; p. 7 altrendo travel/ Getty Images; p. 9 luca amedei/Shutterstock.com; p. 11 Alinari/Getty Images; p. 13 Matej Hudovernik/ Shutterstock.com; p. 15 Thomas McConville/Photographers Choice/Getty Images; p. 17 Hemera Technologies/ Ablestock.com/Thinkstock; p. 19 spirit of america/Shutterstock.com; p. 21 Leemage/Universal Images Group/ Getty Images; p. 23 Amanda Hall/Robert Harding World Imagery/Getty Images.

Library of Congress Cataloging-in-Publication Data

Gaspar, Joe.
  The Statue of Liberty / by Joe Gaspar. — 1st ed.
    p. cm. — (Powerkids readers: American symbols)
  Includes index.
  ISBN 978-1-4777-0735-7 (library binding) — ISBN 978-1-4777-0811-8 (pbk.) —
  ISBN 978-1-4777-0812-5 (6-pack)
  1. Statue of Liberty (New York, N.Y.)—Juvenile literature. 2. New York (N.Y.)—Buildings, structures, etc.—Juvenile literature. I. Title.
  F128.64.L6G38 2014
  974.7'1—dc23
                                        2012043623

Manufactured in the United States of America

CPSIA Compliance Information: Batch #S13PK4: For Further Information contact Rosen Publishing, New York, New York at 1-800-237-9932

CONTENTS

This is the **Statue of Liberty**.

It is tall.

It was a gift from France.

Frédéric Bartholdi designed it.

It was set up in 1886.

Its outside is **copper**.

A steel frame is inside.

It sits on Liberty Island.

This is in New York **Harbor**.

It is fun to visit.

STATUE OF LIBERTY & ELLIS ISLAND

WORDS TO KNOW

copper

harbor

Statue of Liberty

INDEX

WEBSITES

Due to the changing nature of Internet links, PowerKids Press has developed an online list of websites related to the subject of this book. This site is updated regularly. Please use this link to access the list:
www.powerkidslinks.com/pkras/statue/

25